© 2017 Emma Lovett

Acknowledgements

I'd like to thank all those who made this book possible; my friends Lynda and Jenny for accompanying me on some of the walks when Oscar was away, offering suggestions and listening to my ideas; my friend Kris for her input from a hiker's perspective; my friend Lisa for her contacts and my family for providing the space and support to finish this project.

My biggest thanks goes to Oscar - his enduring patience and ability to always get us home was remarkable. By the time we finished the last couple of walks we had the routine down to a tee, with me making the packed lunches and planning the outline route, and him working out the transport to get us there and back, and of course carrying our backpack. I think he asked the question "When is it your turn to carry the bag?" a few hundred times, to which my standard answer was always "On the way back!"

All photographs are the authors' own.

About the authors

Oscar Quiñonez Mayhua is a native Cusqueñan and has lived in Cusco his whole life. He gained his Tourism degree at Tupac Amaru University and is extremely knowledgeable on Inca history and culture. He has over 10 years guiding experience, great local contacts, and knows every inch of the routes in the area.

Emma Lovett has trekked all over the world, from the Himalaya to Alaska, Scotland to the Alps, and of course extensively in Peru and other South American countries. She has lived in Cusco for several years.

Maps and elevation charts

All maps and elevation charts are reproduced with permission from Map My Fitness Inc. I used the Map My Walk app on a smartphone to record all of the hikes.

Introduction

Cusco

Cusco is the heart and capital of the ancient Inca Empire and often referred to as 'the navel of the world' by both its modern day inhabitants and their Incan ancestors. Standing at 3,300m altitude it is surrounded by majestic Andean peaks and fascinating archaeological sites. It was really the discovery of Machu Picchu in 1911 by Hiram Bingham that catapulted Cusco from a quiet backwater town to the tourist mecca it is today. It is visited by hundreds of thousands of tourists every year, and the majority combine a trip to the lost city of the Incas, listed as one of the seven Wonders of the Modern World.

The city itself is a combination of the mighty stone built sloped walls of the Incas and the colonial structures of the invading Spanish. Many of the historic buildings and hotels manage to incorporate both styles. Rarely a week goes by without some sort of street fiesta or parade, mixing the catholic and Inca religions in a flamboyant style for which Latin America is so famous. June 24th sees the biggest celebration of all – Inti Raymi, or Festival of the Sun, where the Inca winter solstice is celebrated, starting at Q'oricancha before the Inca King and Queen lead the revellers up the hill to Sacsayhuaman.

Though the constant urban sprawl now makes it difficult to distinguish, the ninth and perhaps most famous Inca king Pachacuteq designed the city in the shape of the puma, which along with the serpent and the condor were the animal symbols of their religion. At many of the Inca archaeological sites within and surrounding the city, it's possible to see these symbols carved into walls or the worshipping altars, although most were destroyed by the *conquistadors* in an effort to eradicate the Inca religion and superimpose the catholic one.

Close to Cusco lies the Sacred Valley, a lush fertile agricultural area where an abundance of crops are grown, many still using the Inca terraces that reach upwards from the banks of the Urubamba and Vilcanota Rivers. The two major towns in the valley are Pisac and Ollantaytambo both with sizeable Inca sites, bustling craft markets and access to adventure activities such as biking and rafting.

For further information about Cusco, the surrounding area, and the Incas try these books:

Exploring Cusco – Peter Frost

The Conquest of the Incas – John Hemming

Cusco and the Sacred Valley of the Incas - Fernando E. Elorrieta Salazar

Trekking at altitude

The Andes of Peru offer a huge number of trekking and walking holidays through some of the most spectacular scenery in the world. Running the length of South America, with *apus* and peaks at nearly 7000m, and a variety of terrain from glaciers, canyons, lakes and forests, it has all the ingredients to get hikers salivating at the prospect of getting up close and personal to this country.

More than 80% of trekking holidays are taken in the Cusco region, made famous by the Inca Trail trek that runs along the Qhapaq Ñan, the principal Inca Trail which was reserved for the elite Incas who practised spiritual devotion at the numerous sites and *wakas* (worshipping sites) along the way. Due to its increased popularity in recent years, the government of Peru has gradually had to put in restrictions for hiking the Inca Trail, such as advance and limited permits, licensed operators and a checkpoint system along the way. For those hikers or backpackers who haven't booked ahead, there is a decent range of alternative routes, some would argue better, with the same scenery, less crowds, and cheaper prices. All of these multi-day treks finish at Machu Picchu, or other major Inca citadels in the region such as Choquequirao.

All trekking in this region involves being at and hiking at altitude, with the elevation of many of the passes over 4,300m. Arriving in Cusco at 3,300m causes minor problems and breathlessness for most tourists arriving from sea level, or lower altitudes. Generally these last no longer than a couple of days and can be alleviated by following the advice below;

- Rest for a few hours after arrival
- Drink plenty of water and hot tea to avoid dehydration. The local coca tea helps symptoms and is widely available. Avoid alcohol.
- Eat lighter meals, and avoid rich or fatty foods, as your digestion does not work as efficiently at altitude.
- Don't be tempted to over-exert yourself, even if you feel fine.

Paracetamol is usually sufficient to counter mild headaches for most people. For those with concerns that they might become ill whilst on their trek or at higher altitudes, it's usually possible to obtain a prescription for altitude sickness medication prior to your departure. You should discuss with your doctor your individual health and requirements before travelling.

It should be stressed that it is unusual for normal healthy people to suffer from severe altitude sickness. However it is important to be aware that AMS - Acute Mountain Sickness - can occur at any altitude above 2,000m, and in some cases can be life threatening. The risk increases with greater exertion, faster ascents and higher altitudes. Symptoms may include nausea, vomiting, insomnia, dizziness and possibly escalate to pulmonary oedema – fluid on the lungs – or cerebral oedema – swelling of the brain. Altitude sickness medication can help with most symptoms, but the best and sometimes only option is to descend. Travellers should ensure that travel insurance has adequate cover for high altitudes and emergency evacuation.

Inca Trails

The surrounding region of Cusco has many hundreds of kilometres of original Inca trails, laid centuries ago to link the important towns and sites of the Inca Empire. These trails are still in use today by the local population to move goods and livestock between the Andean communities, or, since most people don't own vehicles, to walk to the neighbouring villages. Some are exceptionally well maintained by the National Cultural Institute, the government body responsible for the upkeep and maintenance of historically important sites.

About this guide

This guide contains 16 walks in and around the Cusco area that are ideal for acclimatisation prior to a multi-day trek, or simply for exploring some of the less visited sites in the region. Most include visits to archaeological sites of the Inca era, many of which are overlooked by the tourist dash to Machu Picchu.

Decent topographical maps, like the Ordnance Survey series in the UK, are hard to find, however the walks in this guide have been chosen so that maps are not required, and the use of distance and navigational points make all of these walks navigable for the average hiker.

The walks have all been graded on a scale of Easy, Medium, and Difficult. This is based on an average hiker and assumes little to no acclimatisation beforehand. The actual time taken for the walks are also based on an average hiker, but do not include any extra time taken to view sites, or for normal stops along the way. Variations for personal fitness, stamina, as well as seasonal and weather conditions need to be taken into account. For the longer walks we recommend you start early in the morning, both to avoid walking during the heat of the day, and also to allow yourself spare time to finish walking easily within daylight, although it is relatively safe to travel in the darkness of the early evening. Sunset varies only between the times of 17.30 – 18.15 during the whole year.

Peru has two seasons; the dry season runs from May to September, and the wet season from October to April, the wettest months being January and February. The temperature does not fluctuate much during the year, but allowances need to be made for elevation.

While every care has been taken to ensure the accuracy of the route directions the authors cannot accept responsibility for errors or omissions, or for changes in details given. The countryside is not static, footpaths can be rerouted and changes in ownership can result in paths being closed or diverted.

Hiring a Guide

If you're still not sure about going it alone, or want the peace of mind of an accompanied hike, you can hire a private guide.   Most reputable agencies will arrange this for you, but they will also try to sell you a fixed itinerary tour which means the price will increase. Insist on a private guide only and agree a daily rate – US$20-40 depending on length of day and choice of route. If you hire a guide yourself, make sure they are registered with the AGOTUR - Asociación de Guías Oficiales de Turismo , Association of Official Tour Guides. They have an office in the centre of Cusco and their website is www.agoturcusco.com.pe

Hire the book's guide, Oscar at oscartourleader23@gmail.com.

Getting around

Public transport in Peru is extremely cheap by European/US standards, and buses and *collectivo* taxis run frequently from very early morning to around

9pm at night. Generally there are no timetables for local buses and combis. After that, options are mainly limited to taxis.

Combis – a small bus or minivan running on routes between villages, or on certain routes throughout the city of Cusco. There is a set fare of S/0.70 - 1.00.

Buses – the local buses run from designated places around the city depending on your destination. For the buses needed for the walks in this guide, all the terminals are listed.

Collectivos – small private minivans that run the same routes as the local bus. They are a little more expensive but tend to be much faster. Generally they will depart once they are full, which doesn't take long, but will vary according to the time of day or the popularity of the route. They usually run from the same street as the bus.

Taxis – Taxi travel is also cheap, and for those travellers not on a tight budget, provide a quicker and more direct way to reach the start points or return from the finish points. Fares should always be negotiated in advance, but as a rule, you should allow 3-4 times the price of a bus or *collectivo*. Taxi drivers are knowledgeable about where the bus and collectivo terminals are too.

It is always best to check with your hotel reception, or the taxi driver when heading to a bus or collectivo terminal as the street can and does change without notice, particularly if there is road construction causing delays near the original terminals.

Safety and access

Peru is generally a safe country to travel to and most tourist areas have a highly visible police presence. We recommend you exercise caution though, as tourists (even backpackers) are deemed to be rich by Peruvian standards and as such, are frequently targeted by pickpockets and thieves. Most of the walks in this book are in areas where the local people are used to seeing tourists, however we do not recommend that you hike alone.

While out and about we suggest you leave your passport and the bulk of your money, credit cards etc. in the safe deposit box of your accommodation. Only take with you the money you need to spend and do not display any valuables e.g. a camera around your neck. Carry a photocopy of the picture page of your passport for ID purposes. Make sure your daypack and handbags are secured and never leave them unsupervised.

Whilst it may seem daunting to tackle these walks without the comfort of a map, they are not readily available in Peru, and those that are, are not to a sufficiently detailed scale nor, in some cases, accurate. Most local people are pleased to help tourists find their destinations and start points and you will often find it difficult to extract yourself from a conversation in a local village to begin or continue your hike.

Original Inca trails are publicly accessible to all, but some routes cross private land. Hikers have a responsibility to be sensitive to local farmers and livestock grazing on open land and *altiplanos*.

Personal equipment

Hikers should dress appropriately for the walk they are about to undertake, for example, the walks graded Easy can be done with light trainers/sneakers and light clothing, but hikers should be more prepared for the longer walks. Below is a basic checklist:

- Day Pack
- Hiking boots - for the walks graded Medium to Difficult
- Trekking poles

- Waterproofs
- Compass
- Head lamp or torch - in case of late return
- Camera
- Sunscreen/hat and sunglasses – the sun is extremely strong at altitude. We recommend a minimum of SPF30.
- Personal medical kit, toilet paper, and insect repellent
- Water - the tap water is not safe to drink. Stock up on bottled or filtered water at the start. There are few opportunities to buy water along the routes.
- Snacks or a packed lunch
- Mobile phone for emergencies

Tourist Ticket

The *Boleto Turistico* is available to buy at the Oficina Ejecutiva del Comite inside the Municipalidad on Avenida Sol, the tourist office, or some of the major sites. It costs about S/130, is valid for 10 days from the date of purchase, and gives you access to most of the major sites within the local area. Recently the authorities have increased the entrance price to single sites to S/75, making the ticket good value for money if you wish to visit more than one. The drawback is that you can only visit each site once. Not all of the sites in this book are covered by the *boleto turistico*, but those that aren't usually have smaller and affordable entrance fees.

Bugs and Beasties

In our time hiking the worst injuries we have sustained have usually been self-inflicted, like dehydration, grazed knees from a fall, or a twisted ankle. Having delicate juicy flesh, I have also been bitten a thousand times more than Oscar by mosquitos, which flourish at lower altitudes. It is highly unlikely that you will encounter any of the other nasties along the way as most creatures will make themselves scarce as you approach, but there are a number of bugs and beasties that you should be aware of;

Puma – the lion which inhabits the high plains and mountains, but rarely seen near populated areas or urban districts.

Snakes, spiders and scorpions – More common at the lower altitudes, sweep the area before sitting down to enjoy your picnic!

Feedback

Finally, we would love to hear from you if you have used this guide. We want to hear from you if you have any suggestions on how the directions or contents of any of these walks could be improved, or if there is a walk missing that you'd particularly like included. Any feedback is welcome and we will try to incorporate it into the next edition. Please email us at hikeperu@gmail.com.

Walk Index			
Walk Number	**Walk Name**	**Grade**	**Distance**
1	City walk	Easy	5km/1½hrs
2	Abra Corao to Cusco	Easy	7km/2hrs
3	Huayrapunco to Temple of the Moon	Easy	7½km/2½hrs
4	Ñaupa Iglesia Ñaupa Iglesia and the rock paintings	Easy Easy	7km/2hrs 11km/3½hrs
5	Pumamarca	Easy	8km/2½hrs
6	Tambomachay to Cristo Blanco	Easy	6km/2hrs
7	Lake Huaypo	Medium	12km/4hrs
8	Chinchero to Huallyabamba	Medium	12km/4hrs
9	Devil's Balcony	Medium	7½km/4hrs

10	Inca quarries at Ollantaytambo	Medium	15km/5hrs
11	Lamay to Huchuy Qosqo	Medium	7½km/5hrs
12	Moray and Marinas salt flats	Medium	12km/3hrs
13	Tauca to Huchuy Qosqo	Difficult	16km/7hrs
14	Perilniyoq Waterfall Circuit	Difficult	21km/7hrs
15	Señor de Huanca	Difficult	15km/8hrs
16	Tambomachay to Huchuy Qosqo	Difficult	23km/8hrs
17	Secret way to Machu Picchu for under $50		

Walk Title:	1. City Walk					
Summary:	An easy walk around the central historic part of the city passing some of the most popular visitor attractions. Allow a whole day if you want to incorporate a visit to each of these landmarks.					
Elevation:	Ascent	65m	Descent	65m	Maximum	3,400m
Distance:	5km					
Approx. time:	1½hrs					
Grading:	Easy					
Type:	Circular					
Travelling time:	None					
Entrance fees:	Optional					
Start point:	Plaza de Armas, Cusco					
To get to the start point:	N/A					

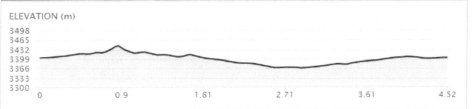

Start in the plaza in the left hand corner as you are facing the cathedral at the palace of the Inca Roq'a. Walk along the side of the plaza to the palace of Pachacuteq and turn right into Plateros. Plateros turns into Saphi, walk another block past the police station and turn right into the alley Amorguru. Head up the steps until you reach the main road. Turn right and in 50m reach the entrance to San Cristobal church and to the right of this the ruins of the palace of Manqo Qhapaq. After exploring these sites, pick up Arco Iris opposite, walk 1½ blocks then turn left into Waynapata and right into

Pumakurko then arrive at the Plaza Nazarenas, where the Nazarenas convent, St Anthony Abbot church, the 5* Belmond Palacio Nazarenas hotel, and several good restaurants are situated.

On the corner of the church is a pedestrian alleyway called Siete Cualebras (Seven Snakes) and you can see these carved into the wall. Walk through the alleyway and turn right onto Choquechaca. At the small crossroads turn left and walk up the small steep road to arrive at San Blas Plazoleta. The church here is worth a visit just to see the amount of amazing gold gilt on display. The plazoleta is a popular starting point for any night out too, as it, and the street behind – Tandapata - host an array of small eateries and bars.

Carry on down Carmen Bajo and turn right, after a few metres cross over the road into a little stepped alley, then turn left into Avenida Tullumayu. Walk down to the large crossroads and see the Handicraft market on your left. This is a great place for souvenir shopping as it has some of the most competitive prices in town.

Turn sharp right at the fountains up into Avenida El Sol passing the large mural on the right hand side as you go. The mural depicts the rise of the Inca and the Spanish invasion. On your left is the Qosqo Centre of Native Art, where there is a display of traditional dance every night – free entrance, but they will pass a bucket around for tips afterwards!

Carry on up the main street to see the magnificent Qoricancha on the right hand side. This is a must-see site and museum, so turn right up Arrayanalyoq to reach the entrance. Just before the entrance on the left is Pampa del Castillo (Castle Lane) whose name was changed some years ago from Pampa del Castigado (Punishment Street). This is where the Inca were whipped and tortured into following the Catholic faith.

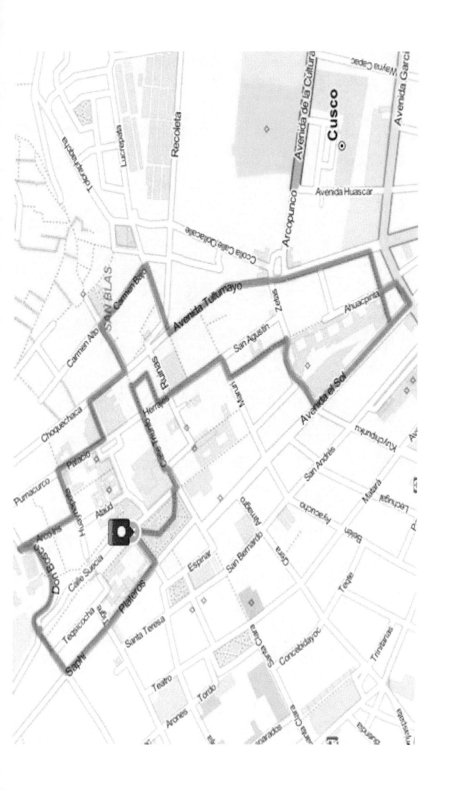

Photo: Qoricancha front entrance

After visiting Qoricancha come out of the entrance, turn right, and then next left up through a pedestrian alleyway past the site Palacio Inka Kusikancha. There are usually some opportunities to have a photo with a dressed-up llama or lamb in this area; S/1 is the target price for you to negotiate! Turn right at the end of the alley and then left into San Agustin. Walk two blocks up past the Marriott hotel, a multi-million dollar spectacular refurbishment of a historic Inca/colonial property to arrive at the corner of the Religious Arts Museum and Herrajes.

Photo: 12-angled stone

Take a detour right here along Hayuta Niloq to see the famous 12-angled stone – one of the best examples of Inca precision stonemasonry.

Back track to the fountain on the corner of Herrajes and follow Samur Wasi back down to the plaza to visit the cathedral.

Photo: Cathedral in Plaza de Armas

Finish point:	Plaza de Armas, Cusco
To return to Cusco:	N/A

Walk Title:	2. Abra Corao to Cusco					
Summary:	An easy walk along an Inca trail which is downhill nearly all the way, so perfect for acclimatisation. Some beautiful views of the Cusco valley, and the route takes you through a small Andean village, and several small Inca sites along the way.					
Elevation:	Ascent	100m	Descent	400m	Maximum	3,725m
Distance:	7km					
Approx. time:	2hrs					
Grading:	Easy					
Type:	Linear					
Travelling time:	30 mins					
Entrance fees:	None					
Start point:	Abra Corao					
To get to the start point:	Take a taxi to Abra Corao which is only 5 mins further on than Tambomachay S/15, or take the bus to Urubamba from Belen Pampa, or the bus to Pisac from Puputi S/1.50 and ask to get off at Abra Corao. Abra Corao is the highest point on the main road (28G) out of Cusco at a junction, there is a small layby with 3 signs; a large blank concrete sign, a medium sized purple INC sign for Sacsayhuaman, and a small old metal sign.					

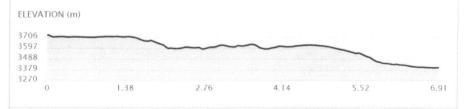

ELEVATION (m)

```
3706
3597
3488
3379
3270
      0        1.38        2.76        4.14        5.52        6.91
```

At the start point face towards Tambomachay and in front of you by the old metal sign find the path that heads downwards in the direction of the village Yuncaypata. After 1km arrive at the village and quickly come to a crossroads in the centre. Go straight ahead to the edge of the village. In front of you is a football pitch, the path continues on the other side, so head around the

right side of the pitch to re-join where it is marked by two mud brick walls either side.

Photo: Cusco

As you pass through the walls there is a vehicle track sweeping away to your left, ignore this and head straight on and soon the path becomes wider. Continue winding along the path for 700m downhill until you reach a green wooden bridge. You will see the valley down on the left hand side. The path now starts to ascend and after 700m you arrive at the ruins of Hacienda Chillkapuyo on your left – there is a barely legible signpost.

Keep to the main path on the left which now continues gradually uphill and starts to level out after 300m, then traverses the valley side until you reach a large orange coloured rock. From here you should see the huge rock that is

the Temple of the Moon 1km directly in front of you. There are a few Inca rocks between now and the Temple. Reach the base of the rock at 4.8km.

Photo: Temple of the Moon

See Temple of the Moon

Continue along the path until you reach the bottom left corner of the Temple. Here, a dirt road travels to your left alongside some houses, but keep to the path that is closest to the Temple and soon it turns into a wide walled grass track.

After 200m arrive at the Temple of the Monkey, also signposted Waka K'usilluchayuo.

See Temple of the Monkey

After a further 700m arrive at the main road up to Sacsayhuaman (28G). If you don't wish to return to the plaza you can flag a taxi or bus from here. Cross the road, and continue down the steps and along the cobbled path for another 800m arriving at the San Blas district. The path now turns into Suyt'uqhatu and then into Calle Plazoleta. Continue downwards, across Choquechaca, and along Hatun Rumiyoc (where the 12 angled stone is) into Triunfo and down to arrive at the plaza.

Finish point:	**Plaza de Armas, Cusco**
To return to Cusco:	N/A

Walk Title:	3. Huayra Punco to Temple of the Moon and Monkey					
Summary:	A pretty walk up through a scenic valley, taking in some of the least visited Inca sites in Cusco and finishing in the Temple of the Moon area.					
Elevation:	Ascent	200m	Descent	180m	Maximum	3,662m
Distance:	7.5km					
Approx. time:	2½hrs					
Grading:	Easy					
Type:	Linear					
Travelling time:	15 mins					
Entrance fees:	None					
Start point:	The INC office on Huayra Punco in the Alto los Incas district					
To get to the start point:	Taxi from the centre S/10. The combi 'Expresso Inka' runs from Rosaspata market/Cultura Avenue right to the INC office. It is the last stop.					

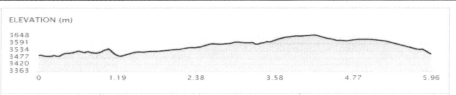

Take the steps down to the right hand side of the INC office and round to the left. Take the level upper path which continues on the left hand side of the valley. On the other side of the valley you can already see the Inca terraces of the Kallachaka site.

Continue on this path for another 2km to reach the site of Inkilltambo. The INC were busy restoring this site when we visited and it is due to be open during 2016.

Photo: terraces at Kallachaka

See Inkilltambo

By the site of Inkilltambo is a small green fenced water reservoir. Walk round the left side of this and pick up the path at the far end, which runs alongside the stream. Continue parallel to the stream and soon cross to the right hand side at the base of a rock with Inca stonework.

Photo: Inca oven at Inkilltambo

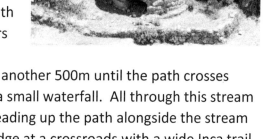

Do not be tempted to follow the path on the left hand side as it soon veers away in a different direction.

Continue on the right hand side for another 500m until the path crosses back over on a natural bridge with a small waterfall. All through this stream and path are queuña trees. Keep heading up the path alongside the stream until you reach a green wooden bridge at a crossroads with a wide Inca trail. Turn left onto this path which is the Qhapaq Nan.

The path now starts to ascend and after 700m you arrive at the ruins of Hacienda Chillkapuyo on your left – there is a barely legible signpost.

At the Hacienda take the upper path (although the lower one will eventually also reach the Temple of the Moon) and head upwards towards a large grey rock.

Photo: Wild lupins

In 500m reach a worship site Wak'a Ch'llkapujio which is signposted. Continue up the now wide path and as you crest the hill you should see the Temple of the Moon a few hundred metres directly in front of you. There are a few small Inca rock structures between now and the Temple.

See Temple of the Moon and Temple of the Monkey

Photo: Temple of the Moon

Continue along the path until you reach the bottom left corner of the Temple. Here, a dirt road travels to your left alongside some houses, but keep to the path that is closest to the Temple and soon it turns into a wide walled grass track. After 150m arrive at the Temple of the Monkey, also signposted Waka K'usilluchayuo. After a further 700m arrive at the main road up to Sacsaywaman. If you don't wish to return to the plaza you can flag a taxi or bus from here.

Cross the road, and continue down the steps. Continue ahead for another 600m arriving at the San Blas district, and on your left find Plazoleta de San Blas. Here continue down Calle Plazoleta, across Choquechaca, and along Hatun Rumiyoc (where the 12 angled stone is) into Triunfo and down to arrive at the plaza.

Finish point:	Plaza de Armas, Cusco
To return to Cusco:	N/A

Walk Title:	4. Ñaupa Iglesia				
Summary:	Part of a larger circuit visiting the beautiful carved stone altar and Inca worshipping site of Ñaupa Iglesia and the rock paintings. For the full circuit see Perilniyoq Waterfall Circuit.				
Elevation:	Ascent	310m	Descent	260m	Maximum	3,100m
Distance:	Opt A: Ñaupa Iglesia only 7km Opt B: Ñaupa Iglesia and the rock paintings 11km				
Approx. time:	Opt A: 2hrs Opt B: 3½hrs				
Grading:	Easy				
Type:	Out and Back				
Travelling time:	70mins each way to Pachar				
Entrance fees:	None				
Start point:	Pachar				
To get to the start point:	Take a collectivo towards Ollantaytambo S/10 and ask to get off at Pachar.				

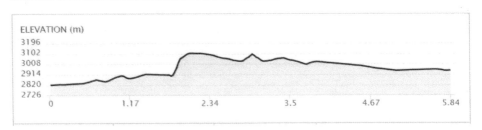

As you get off at Pachar there is a sign with a map of the whole circuit. From here cross the bridge and turn left. Follow the road around and through the small plaza. 500m from the start reach a turn-off where the blue sign indicates to go right for the circuit. Fork left here as the footpath cuts off the corner. At 1.1km the road turns into the path and it runs alongside crop fields and an avocado plantation. The road and railway tracks run out on your right hand side.

At 2km cross over the bridge and turn left, walking along the railway tracks. Although there are only two scheduled trains a day along this part of the railway, care should be taken, and where possible, walk on the path alongside the tracks.

Photo: Huarocondo gorge

After another 600m you reach a railway crossing and the road bridge, from here you can see the agricultural terraces up on the right side of the valley.

Photo: Agricultural terraces and caves

Keep to the railway tracks and in 300m a path leaves the tracks up to your right. Keep on this until you reach a boulder, then turn right to take the stepped and steep path up through the middle of the terraces. The site is not maintained at all, so be careful of loose rocks.

Make your way over to the large overhanging rock to see the small niches, which were probably positioned to catch the sun at the solstices. The carved altar of the *waka* is in the cave behind this rock. The three steps carved into the altar represent the three worlds; the Underworld, the Living World, and the Celestial World.

Photo: Carved altar at Ñaupa Iglesia

For **Option** A, retrace your steps all the way to Pachar.

Option **B**, go back to the bridge and cross over to pick up the vehicle track. Walk along the track for another 2km until you reach the rock paintings which are across from the river. It's possible to walk along the railway tracks to the paintings, as you can get closer to them, but for safety reasons it's not recommended.

Photo: Rock paintings

Retrace your steps back to Pachar.

Finish point:	Pachar
To return to Cusco:	Flag down any bus or collectivo to Cusco, or Urubamba bus terminal then take a bus or collectivo from Urubamba back to Cusco.

Walk Title:	5. Pumamarca						
Summary:	Pumamarca, which translates to 'print of the puma' sits on a hillside overlooking the rivers Río Patacancha and the Yuracmayo. This well-preserved site was thought to be a military outpost and control point for access to Ollantaytambo. There are two options available to reach Pumamarca.						
Elevation:	Ascent	230m	Descent	750m	Maximum	3,380m	
Distance:	Option A: 8km Option B: 13km						
Approx. time:	Option A: 2½hrs Option B: 6hrs						
Grading:	Option A: Easy Option B: Medium						
Type:	Option A: Linear Option B: Out and Back						
Travelling time:	1½hrs each way to Ollantaytambo, 15mins to Pallata						
Entrance fees:	None						
Start point:	Option A: Pallata Option B: Ollantaytambo plaza						
To get to the start point:	Take a collectivo from Pavitos to Ollantaytambo S/10. For **Option A** take a combi S/1 or a mototaxi S/15 towards Patacancha and get off at Pallata.						

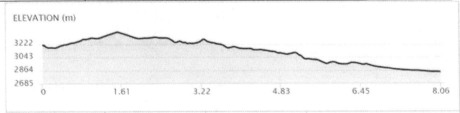

This route follows **Option A**, but for **Option B**, simply follow the route in reverse. It is also possible to get a mototaxi all the way up to Pumamarca, but when we asked around the taxi drivers were asking around S/50 for the trip.

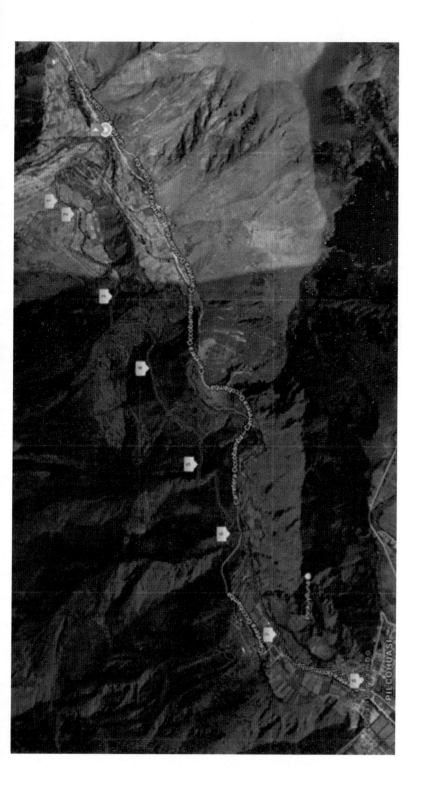

Pallata is a small community about 5km out of Ollantaytambo on the Patacancha road. Get out at the signpost for the village and next to the INC sign. Head down through the houses and cross the river. Turn left, cross the second wooden bridge and head up to your right to soon reach the new footbridge. Turn sharp left here and follow the path up the hill.

At 500m reach the vehicle track, turn right and in a few metres turn left again onto the path. This soon follows a stream and water channel upstream.

Photo: Inca aqueducts

When you reach the vehicle track again, turn left and follow the track over a wooden bridge until you reach an electricity junction and pylon number 32992 by some boulders. Turn right and follow the path for 400m up through the terraces until you reach Pumamarca site.

See Pumamarca

After visiting the site, retrace your steps back down to the vehicle track to the electricity junction. Turn right along the track and in 200m reach a small wooden sign for a campsite and Ollantaytambo. Walk on beyond the sign one field and turn left so you are parallel with the track. Climb over the stile and the path is marked with stones for a while.

Cross over a water channel and down to your left you have great views of the valley below.

Continue on down the path near to the water channel and after 500m reach some small waterfalls. After another couple of hundred metres you enter the huge agricultural terraces which surround this area, and should see another wooden sign.

Photo: Agricultural terraces

Carry on down the path for another 2km, passing a blue water tank, and eventually reach the road that runs through Media Luna. Turn right along the road and in 100m veer left to pick up the path that runs behind the houses and alongside the river. When you reach the road again, turn left,

cross the bridge and pass by the hostel Mama Simona. Follow the road down, and in 100m turn left into Patacalle, the ancient road that runs outside the wall of Ollantaytambo.

Photo: Patacalle in Ollantaytambo

Continue right to the end and then turn left to arrive back at the plaza.

Finish point:	Ollantaytambo plaza

To return to Cusco:	Collectivos S/10 back to Cusco run from or near the plaza.

Walk Title:	6. Tambomachay to Cristo Blanco				
Summary:	This downhill walk is a great replacement for the traditional city tour which takes in these popular Inca sites close to Cusco. Take your time at each site instead of being herded on and off the bus.				
Elevation:	Ascent	<50m	Descent	380m	Maximum	3,780m
Distance:	6km				
Approx. time:	2hrs				
Grading:	Easy				
Type:	Linear				
Travelling time:	20mins				
Entrance fees:	**Tourist ticket required to enter all the sites, or none if you bypass them.**				
Start point:	Tambomachay				
To get to the start point:	Tambomachay is on the outskirts of town as you leave the Sacsayhuaman site. Take a taxi from the centre S/15, or take the Señor de Huerto bus to the final stop on its route S/1.20				

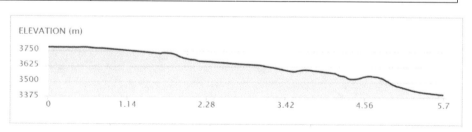

From Tambomachay head back down towards Puca Pucara on the path that runs alongside the road.

After 600m past the layby at the site, pick up the track that veers off left before you reach the village of Huayllarcocha.

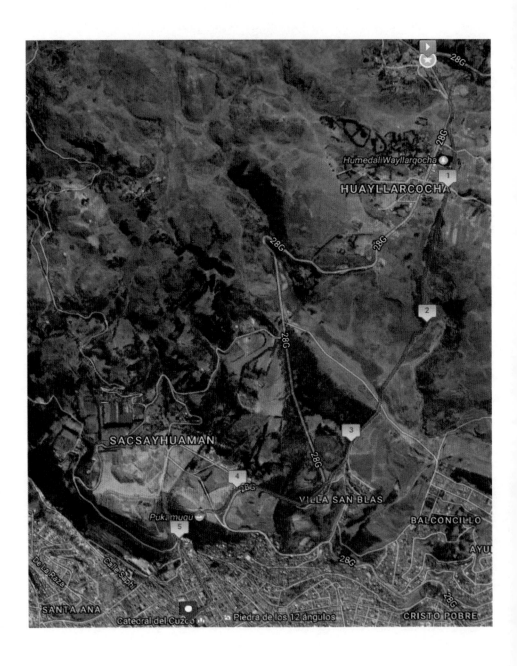

Photo: Puca Pucara

Follow the path to the left hand side of the lake and along the barbed wire fence. Here you can see parts of the original Quepac Ñan though it hasn't been restored. Carry on past the football pitch crossing a concrete water channel running from the lake. Just past 1km the path starts to descend down into a valley by a band of eucalyptus trees, and after 700m there is a large rock on your right.

Here, the path bends round to the left, but cross the marshy area and pick up the path that runs along the right hand side.

Photo: Large rock in the valley

At 2km you can see Inca ruins down to your left which have been partially restored. Keep heading down the path crossing another marshy area until at 2.8km you reach a vehicle track. Turn left here for the short detour here if you want to visit the Temple of the Moon. Cross the vehicle track to pick up the other track running up ahead frequented by the horse riding tours in the area.

Continue along this track for another 300m to reach a concrete road. Follow this around to the right to reach the site of Q'enqo.

Photo: Q'enqo

Walk along the road (there is a wide verge) back down towards Sacsayhuaman and on your left you can see Cristo Blanco. Head towards the statue which was built by a group of Christian Palestinians that were seeking refuge in Cusco in 1945. Walk in front of the statue and out through the small parking space, down into the dip and turn left to pick up the path that brings you out to the Sacsayhuaman control booth.

From here you can head down the staircase, along Calle Palacio, turn right at Plazoleta de las Nazarenas and reach the Plaza in 2 blocks.

Finish point:	Plaza de Armas, Cusco
To return to Cusco:	n/a

Walk Title:	7. Lake Huaypo						
Summary:	This walk is great for acclimatisation as it is at a higher elevation than Cusco, but is an easy level walk round one of the prettiest lakes in the area. A fantastic opportunity too, to interact with the local farmers on the shores, as they are eager to share stories and knowledge of the lake. Good for bird watching as well.						
Elevation:	Ascent	130m	Descent	130m	Maximum	3,600m	
Distance:	12km						
Approx. time:	4hrs						
Grading:	Medium						
Type:	Circular						
Travelling time:	45mins						
Entrance fees:	None						
Start point:	Lake Huaypo						
To get to the start point:	Take a bus towards Urubamba and ask to get off at Huaypo. From there either walk (1km) or take a moto taxi down the main road through Huaypo to the lake.						

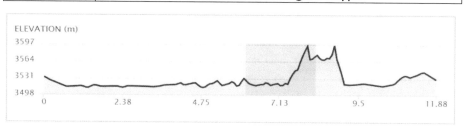

You are simply circumnavigating the lake. There is a vehicle track three quarters of the way round and at the time of writing construction was underway to complete the track circuit.

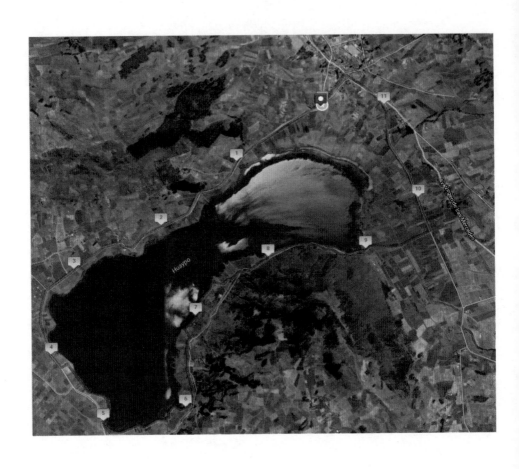

It's not possible to walk completely all the way round the lake on the shores,

but some of it is, and there are small paths through the crop fields and the paths used by the pastors to move the animals.

Photo: potato crops on the lake shore

About half way round there is a very basic campsite with seating which makes a good place to picnic.

Try to take the time to speak to the farmers and fishermen on the shores, they are friendly and very keen to show you their way of life.

Photo: Harvesting reeds for fishing rafts or cow fodder

When the road runs out on the far side, make your way through the crop fields back towards the village. There are numerous small paths and animal tracks you can follow.

Finish point:	Lake Huaypo
To return to Cusco:	Walk or taxi back to the main road and flag any collectivo or bus heading back to Cusco. There are plenty.

Walk Title:	8. Chinchero to Huayllabamba					
Summary:	Starting in the pretty town of Chinchero famous for its weaver women, a beautiful downhill walk through a quiet canyon and along the Qhapaq Ñan Inca trail, arriving at the small village of Urquillos then along the banks of the Rio Vilcanota to Huayllabamba. A traditional market is held on a Tuesday, Thursday and Sunday.					
Elevation:	Ascent	<50m	Descent	940m	Maximum	3,745m
Distance:	12km					
Approx. time:	4hrs					
Grading:	Medium					
Type:	Linear					
Travelling time:	30mins to Chinchero, 1hr return from Huayllabamba					
Entrance fees:	None					
Start point:	Chinchero market square					
To get to the start point:	Take a bus bound for Urubamba from Belen Pampa S/3 or a collectivo S/4 from the same street and get off at Chinchero central. It's a 5 minute walk from there to the market square.					

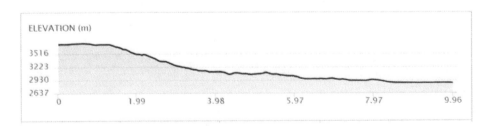

ELEVATION (m)

3516					
3223					
2930					
2637					
0	1.99	3.98	5.97	7.97	9.96

From the entrance to the market square, head towards the public toilets on the left hand side, and out through the stone arch. Ahead of you is a sign showing the part of Qhapaq Ñan the route follows.

Soon reach the INC sign at the edge of the archaeological site. Veer right to follow the path to Urquillos and continue past the Inca terraces. You will need a Boleto Turistico to visit the complete site.

Photo: terraces at Chinchero

At 1km you reach the end of the walls and start down the steps into a tree-lined valley. The path is very well maintained and obvious all the way now to the end. Continue down the valley on the right hand side of the stream and after 800m reach a junction. Turn left here. After another 400m arrive at the foundations of Q'entecapilla, the Hummingbird Chapel. At the time of writing the only remains of the sign here was the concrete block. This makes a great mirador though, as you have views down the canyon to The Sacred Valley.

See Sacred Valley

Photo: The Qhapaq Ñan with Mt Pitursiray in the distance

At 2.5km another missing sign concrete block points the way to the Pop Pop waterfall. This is a 600m down and back up optional detour. Head to the right on the 4th left hand switchback. The written route has not counted this detour in distances and timings.

1.6km on from the waterfall turn-off you arrive at a grassy area which makes a good spot for a picnic. Continue down the main path and into a wooded area until after 1km you reach a clearing in the trees with a signpost for Uran Mayu. There is a small stone marker on the ground, so turn left towards Urquillos, cross over stream on the small wooden bridge, and pick up the path heading out right.

After another 1km reach the small chapel at Erapata Cabracancha, and in a further 500m the path joins the vehicle track.

Photo: Chapel

It's another 1.5km from this point into Urquillos. The plaza and church are on your right, and it might be possible to get transport out from here, but it's easier from Huayllabamba. Keep on the vehicle track out past the village and after a few hundred metres you see the complex of Hotel Aranwa on your right, soon passing its large wooden gates. You are now alongside the river Vilcanota which you follow all the way into the village of Huayllabamba. Turn right to cross the bridge and after 300m reach the main road.

Finish point:	Huayllabamba
To return to Cusco:	Jump on a combi towards Urubamba (10 mins) and get off at or near the bus terminal. Buses S/4 and collectivos S/5 both run from here back to Cusco.

Walk Title:	9. Devil's Balcony						
Summary:	This walk takes you over the back hills of Cusco to the region of Chacan, for a quiet escape from the city noise, and some pretty scenery. Chacan was an Inca worship site, and the Devil's Balcony (Balcon del Diablo) is a remarkable coloured cliff face with a small cave entrance, and a cave window.						
Elevation:	Ascent	230m	Descent	315m	Maximum	3,785m	
Distance:	7.5km						
Approx. time:	4hrs						
Grading:	Medium						
Type:	Circular						
Travelling time:	15 mins each way						
Entrance fees:	None						
Start point:	Control booth at the back of Sacsayhuaman (the coach park), Cusco						
To get to the start point:	The Señor de Huerto bus will take you up to the large field behind Cristo Blanco and from there you can walk across 400m to the control booth.						

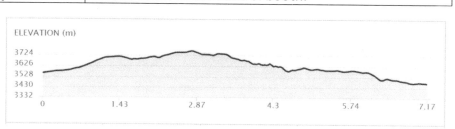

From the control booth, and with Cristo Blanco behind you, look up to the hill to see the purple INC sign. Head towards this.

If you have a ticket for the Sacsayhuaman complex you can go straight across the field (the rangers are strict at this site). If you don't, you can walk in a straight line from the post along the paved road adjacent a small field.

At the large white building on the corner turn left along a small path with stream and left again at the next corner. Follow the path up through the rocks and veer right at the top.

Photo: Sacsayhuaman

The INC sign is signposted left to Chacan and straight ahead to Huchuy Qosqo. Even though the sign says left, go straight ahead as this is a prettier route.

After a few metres a large grey granite shale pyramid can be seen over to the right. Carry on up through the eucalyptus trees for another 300m to see an overhanging rock on your left. Continue another 400m upwards to reach the crest of the hill. Here you can either continue for another 400m straight ahead on the path, then turn left at the lumpy hill to pick up the track, or veer left across the field heading towards the red slate rooftop of the lone farmhouse. Pass by on the track with the farmhouse to your left.

A little further down there are two small terraced lakes to your right (these may be empty during dry season) and continue down the track. Soon reach the edge of the village and a T junction. Here you should see the start of a concrete water channel. Turn right here, and follow the path up through the village for another 150m. The water channel crosses in front of you, turn left at the corner of the house and follow the path alongside the water channel. You follow this water channel all the way to Chacan with little to no deviation.

Continuing along the path beside the channel, your path ascends gently up and round to pass another lone building on your left. Soon, the channel becomes unconcreted, and you are now at the top side of a valley down to your left. Pass by another large farmhouse and pick up the widened path. This is a common route used by locals, is well trodden, and you may see livestock along the way. After 400m arrive at the natural rock bridge over the Devil's Balcony. The water channel is running directly along this bridge now. To your left you should be able to see directly down the valley, with the stream below you. To your right you should see some Inca agricultural terracing. Head down to the right to explore the Chacan area, and the caves. If you have time there are lots of ruins in this area. Take care in the caves, especially during rainy season when the water levels are higher.

Photo: Devil's Balcony

When you are ready to leave, head back up to the rock bridge and look down the valley. At the V end of the valley you can see a eucalyptus wood, which you are heading for. Walk out opposite to the way you came, and soon reach a fork with three paths. The two better paths lead only up to the village. Take the third lowest path. The path traverses a small crop area, and round towards the left through an area of rocks, keeping them on your left. About 400m from the fork you should see a large Inca wall on your right. Pass by the wall and out again to your left.

Generally this path now descends on the outer edge of the valley down towards the V.

After 200m there is a small set of switchbacks, and soon you descend you enter a queuña grove (1km from the balcony) and after another 100m the path crosses a dug water channel again.

Photo: queuña tree

From here you can see a large rounded rock on the bottom opposite side of the valley, and this is where you need to cross the river. Follow the path down, but do not be tempted to head straight for the rock, as there are some steep edges. If you find it difficult to spot the path here (frequent animal tracks blur the footpath), you should have a line of eucalyptus in front of you, and the path eventually becomes clearer and runs parallel to these. Descend steeply to the river and cross. This is easy enough in dry season but poles are a help in rainy season.

In front of you are signs of an Inca wall, climb up and out to the right to

arrive at the eucalyptus wood. Here there is a clear wide flat forest track which you follow out. After 750m arrive at a small clearing where another forest track merges from the right.

Photo: Clearing in eucalyptus wood

Continue along the track until you reach the Incatambo hotel – the building was constructed in memory of the granddaughter of Spanish conqueror Francisco Pizarro - on your left hand side. The path becomes cobbled and after 400m reach the junction with the main road. There is another purple Sacsayhuaman INC sign at this junction. To return to your start point, turn left here (you will need your ticket again) or to return to town turn right. Follow the main road down the hill until you reach the main pedestrian entrance and control booth to Sacsayhuaman and another INC sign.

Finish point:	Front control booth of Sacsayhuaman, Cusco
To return to Cusco:	To return to the centre of town, take any staircase down from the front control booth, or hail a taxi.

Walk Title:	10. Inca Quarries and Sun Gate					
Summary:	This easy to navigate route follows a well-preserved Inca trail to Cachiccata, the site of the stone quarries (canteras) used for the construction of Ollantaytambo. The quarries are still littered with carved and chiselled rocks that were half-finished and which never made it to their destination.					
Elevation:	Ascent	800m	Descent	800m	Maximum	3,519m
Distance:	15km					
Approx. time:	5hrs					
Grading:	Medium – quarries only Difficult – Sun Gate					
Type:	Circular					
Travelling time:	1.5hrs each way					
Entrance fees:	None					
Start point:	Ollantaytambo					
To get to the start point:	Take a collectivo from Pavitos S/10 to Ollantaytambo					

Author's note: I have walked this route three times at different times of the year, and it has always been blazing hot. Wear a sun-hat and take plenty of water as there is none on the way round.

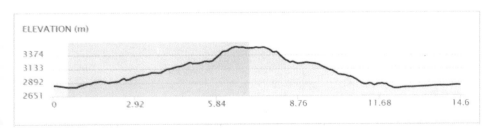

From the plaza, exit towards the market, turn right then immediately left. At the end of the street, head down the steps and through the tunnel under the road into the town. Turn right and soon reach the corner. Here the

quarry route is signposted – Canteras de Cachiccata. Head down the track and cross over the Inca bridge (although it has largely been replaced with modern materials) and directly in front of you is a large map.

Photo: Map at Inca bridge

Turn right after the bridge and follow the gradual ascent parallel to the river. At 2km you reach a fork in the path where *Canteras* is painted onto a rock. Keep left here to continuing ascending. After another 1.6km you reach some small stone ruins and agricultural terraces. Reach mirador Pacareqtampu and shelter at 4.3km then the first camping site at 5.7km. Just after the campsite is the first quarry and the *chullpas* stone burial towers.

Photo: Chullpas

About 100m further on from the first quarry there is another fork. This is your return point. To visit the second quarry and sun gate take the left fork uphill through the switchbacks for 1.6km. As the path levels out the second quarry is on your left. This one contains needle shaped blocks whose use is unknown.

Photo: chiselled rock

This route does not include the Sun Gate (Inti Punku) but if you wish to visit it too, allow another 1½ hours there and 1 hour back. From the path through the quarry, look up to the ridge ahead to see the Sun Gate. Find the large boulder with INC painted on it and pick up the path on the left of it. Follow it uphill crossing scree and reach a grass field and some ruins. Beyond these, the path continues, then fork right at a small ravine to reach the Sun Gate after another few hundred metres. Mt Salkantay can be seen through the gate. Return back along the same route to reach the return point just after the first quarry.

Turn sharp left at the return point to re-join the circular path and soon arrive at the second larger campsite with toilet facilities (not always open). Walk through the campsite and pick up the path on the other side, and follow the gradual switchbacks down. Note though, that the path heads away from Ollantaytambo for a short while before switching back towards the town.

Photo: View of The Sacred Valley

After 1km you reach a smallholding which is on the outskirts of the Cachiccata village. Turn left down some grassy steps, parallel to the stream and cross a tiny bridge. Continue down through the village and at the corner the path turns into vehicle track. Follow the track out of the village and cross the bridge.

There are a couple of options to return to the town centre, either turn immediately right to follow the road along the railroad tracks, or slightly further ahead, turn right to pick up the road which comes into the back of town. There is little difference in the distances, but taking the second option it's possible to flag down a minivan for a lift the last kilometre or two back into town.

Finish point:	Ollantaytambo plaza
To return to Cusco:	Take a collectivo from just off the plaza S/10.

Walk Title:	11. Lamay to Huchuy Qosqo						
Summary:	An easy to navigate hike that ascends from the town of Lamay up to the archaeological complex of Huchuy Qosqo. This is the shortest and easiest route to Huchuy Qosqo, although the gradient and out and back route makes it the least interesting way to reach it.						
Elevation:	Ascent	690m	Descent	690m	Maximum	3,640m	
Distance:	7.5km						
Approx. time:	5hrs						
Grading:	Medium						
Type:	Out and back						
Travelling time:	1 hour each way						
Entrance fees:	Huchuy Qosqo S/10						
Start point:	Lamay						
To get to the start point:	Take the bus or collectivo from Calle Puputi towards Urubamba/Calca, and get off at Lamay.						

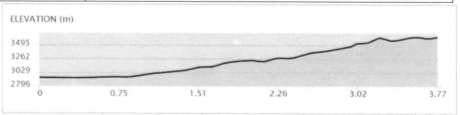

From the bus stop in Lamay, outside the covered market area, look across the road for the red INC sign. Cross the main road and head down the paved road. After 200m cross the bridge and follow the road around to the right towards the village.

Turn left through the village past the restaurant and start heading upwards. There are several routes to reach the Inca trail so don't worry which one you choose. Once at the top of the village, the trail to Huchuy Qosqo is signposted, and the trail runs out towards the right, up the hill. At the time of writing the vehicle track was being extended and the beginning of the footpath was cordoned off. However, there were a couple of alternatives available and as long as your direction is up and to the right, it is difficult to get lost. Once back on the main trail, it is easy to follow, well used and maintained, and ascends gradually along the valley side. There is only one fork to the left near the top, which you should ignore. Soon the trail becomes steeper and into switchbacks for the last 100m ascent. Once you reach the top, the trail traverses round to the right on the level, and continue along this path for another 500m to reach the complex of Huchuy Qosqo. A ranger will usually find you while you're looking round the site to ask for your entrance fee. After spending time at the site, retrace your footsteps to return the way you came.

Finish point:	Lamay
To return to Cusco:	The bus stop is immediately adjacent to the red INC sign. Buses to Cusco run approx. every 15 minutes S/3, or hail a collectivo from the same place S/5.

Walk Title:	12. Moray and the Maras salt flats					
Summary:	A beautiful downhill walk starting from the Inca site of Moray, through the working salt mines of Maras and finishing in Urubamba.					
Elevation:	**Ascent**	**<50m**	**Descent**	**700m**	**Maximum**	**3,520m**
Distance:	**12km**					
Approx. time:	**3hrs**					
Grading:	**Medium**					
Type:	**Linear**					
Travelling time:	**75mins to Moray, 1hr return from Urubamba**					
Entrance fees:	**Moray S/70 or included on the turistico boleto, Maras S/10**					
Start point:	**Moray**					
To get to the start point:	Take a bus from Belen Pampa S/4, or collectivo from Pavitos S/7 towards Urubamba and get off at the Moray/Maras turn. Taxis wait at this junction to take passengers to Moray S/15.					

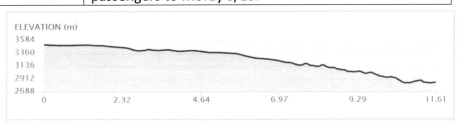

After exploring the Moray complex *(see Moray)* head out of the site back on the vehicle track. After 500m on a corner pick up the wide footpath that leaves the track to the left and soon reach a weathered INC sign for Pacallamayo. Take the left fork shortly afterwards and now your route to Maras should be marked with white arrows.

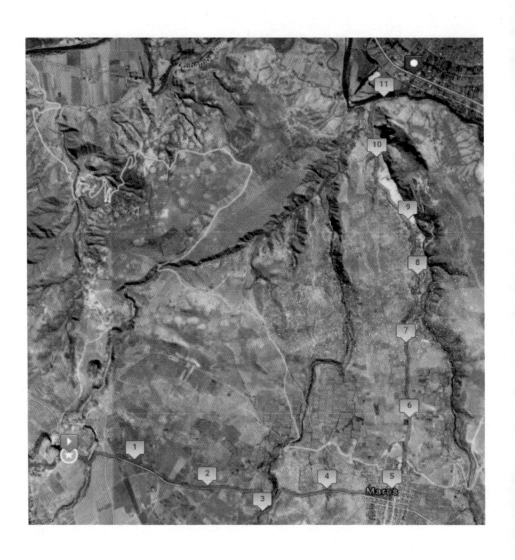

After exploring the Moray complex *(see Moray)* head out of the site back on the vehicle track. After 500m on a corner pick up the wide footpath that leaves the track to the left and soon reach a weathered INC sign for Pacallamayo. Take the left fork shortly afterwards and now your route to Maras should be marked with white arrows.

At 1.7km the path goes between a small reservoir and a small pond and heads off left past an old adobe brick house. Now you should see the town of Maras straight ahead.

The path continues downwards and loops in and out of a small ravine and at 4.3km you reach the outskirts of town, with the new red school building outside the walls.

Photo: Ravine at Maras

Continue into town and take the 4th left to arrive at the plaza at 5.1km. Here you can have a basic meal or stock up on snacks and water. Head diagonally across the plaza to the red building (toilets) on the corner and follow the road heading out of town. After 350m take the path off the road where there is an INC sign. Head directly straight, there are several forks and turn offs but ignore these, and pass under electricity lines. This is a popular route for mountain bikers who descend this path at a rate of knots, so be careful to allow them space.

At 7.1km the path splits, take the upper left hand one, although the lower path converges further on it is less well maintained.

After another 1km you should start to see the salt flats below you. Continue down the path to arrive at the entrance at 9km. Here you can buy snacks, water and souvenirs and there was a restaurant under construction at the time of writing.

The salt pans, or salineras, at Maras date from pre-Inca times and are individually owned by the people of Maras and Pichingoto. The flow of the salty stream from the mine is redirected every few days to ensure that every person's pan is replenished fairly. The best time to visit is during dry season (June-August) when the salt is a brilliant white and the appearance is of icy geometric structures.

There is a path through the salt pans on the left hand side although it is very narrow on some parts, the illusion of ice from the salt and the small drops either side can make it disorientating for some. After 700m pick up the vehicle track coming down from your left hand side and soon turn left to pick up the well maintained path again. The path runs down and through the small community of Pichingoto eventually meeting the Urubamba river. At 11.1km cross over the river and head in a straight direction through the few houses to meet the main road after 500m.

Finish point:	Urubamba
To return to Cusco:	Flag down any bus/collectivo returning to Cusco, or a combi to take you to nearby Urubamba bus terminal. From there you can travel by bus or collectivo directly back to Cusco.

Walk Title:	**13. Tauca to Huchuy Qosqo**
Summary:	This walk, although physically difficult, is very easy to navigate, following a well-marked Inca trail the entire way. A gradual ascent up through a valley, to arrive at a beautiful altiplano with grazing llamas. Then descending towards the Sacred Valley and the archaeological complex of Huchuy Qosqo, before finishing on the valley floor in Lamay.

Elevation:	Ascent	400m	Descent	1,700m	Maximum	4,400m

Distance:	16km
Approx. time:	7hrs
Grading:	Difficult
Type:	Linear
Travelling time:	1 hour each way
Entrance fees:	Huchuy Qosqo S/25
Start point:	Tauca
To get to the start point:	Take a collectivo from Belen Pampa to Chinchero and get off at the Alpachaca turn, at the beginning of the village at the taxi rank – S/3. Then take a taxi to Tauca S/10 per car. The start point is an INC sign to Huchuy Qosqo. You might be able to persuade the driver to take you further down this track road to reduce the amount of uphill walking.

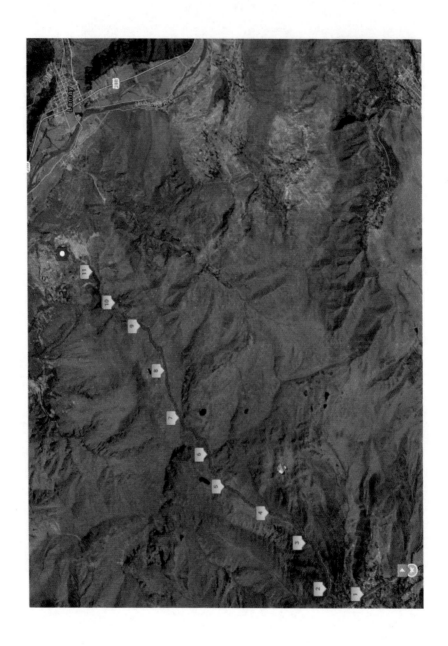

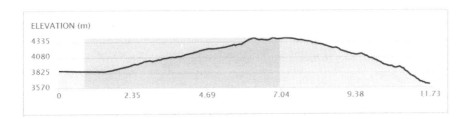

ELEVATION (m)

From Tauca, follow the track road up and out of the village and very soon you will start into the valley.

Photo: Lake Piuray behind you near the start

The track ascends gradually up through the valley and after a while the Inca trail starts alongside and runs parallel. At 4.5km on the left is a large dirt area that the vehicles use to turn in. (Your taxista may bring you as far as here). From here the trail becomes grassier and skirts around the right hand side of the valley. You are heading towards the small U indent in the ridge.

Photo: Ascending the valley

The trail turns to dirt, and there are a few switchbacks to take you up to the first pass, eventually levelling out at 2 large cairns of stones at 6km. These mark the top of the pass (4,400m). To the right of the pass is a beautiful altiplano, with several lakes and herds of llama grazing.

Photo: Grazing llamas

Continue along the trail, which traverses round the left hand side of the altiplano for another 600m to reach the second pass (4,400m) marked by smaller piles of stones. From here descend on the trail down into a small valley until the vegetation starts to become thicker.

Photo: The trail from the second pass

At 9.5km you should see a large pinkish cliff face to your left and soon the Inca agricultural terraces of the Huchuy Qosqo complex start. After a few more metres you arrive at a stream, and the complex is now signposted, the path stays close to the stream for a while. At 10km you should get your first glimpse of the complex below you. Continue another 1km down the trail towards it. There is no entry gate, the ranger will find you to ask for entrance fees.

Photo: Huchuy Qosqo

Head out of the complex on the right hand corner and pick up the trail again towards Lamay, signposted. The trail continues steeply down a number of switchbacks before the gradient eases for a gentler descent. Follow the trail all the way to the small village at the bottom, and head out the right side on the paved road towards the bridge. Cross the bridge and in another 200m arrive at the main road in Lamay.

Finish point:	Lamay
To return to Cusco:	The bus stop is immediately adjacent to the finish point. Buses to Cusco are approx. every 15 minutes – S/2, or hail a collectivo - S/5. A taxi all the way back to Cusco will cost S/35.

Walk Title:	14. Perolniyoq Waterfall Circuit					
Summary:	A circuit visiting the Inca worshipping site of Ñaupa Iglesia, the rock paintings, the small community of Soccma, Perolniyoq waterfall and the Inca ruins at Raqaypata and Chocana. The stiff climb up to Soccma is rewarded with stunning views of the Sacred Valley below.					
Elevation:	Ascent	1,340m	Descent	440m	Maximum	3,730m
Distance:	21km					
Approx. time:	6-8hrs					
Grading:	Difficult					
Type:	Circular					
Travelling time:	70mins each way to Pachar					
Entrance fees:	None					
Start point:	Pachar					
To get to the start point:	Take a collectivo towards Ollantaytambo S/10 and ask to get off at Pachar.					

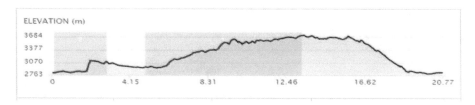

As you get off at Pachar there is a sign with a map of the whole circuit. It should be noted that this map is not to scale and gives a rather misleading idea of the length of the second half and uppermost part of the hike. The distance is only shown for a couple of parts, with timings shown instead.

Follow the **Ñaupa Iglesia and rock paintings** walk in this book. From the rock paintings carry on along the vehicle track until you reach a bridge and junction signposted to Soccma.

Cross over the bridge and turn left up the footpath that runs alongside a stream and through some houses. This path cuts off the corner and you soon meet up with the vehicle track again. The vehicle track zig zags up the hill to arrive at Soccma, and the footpath crosses the track a number of times, and is fairly easy to find, and of course, a much more pleasant walk than the track.

Soccma is approx. 2km from the bridge crossing. Just before you enter into the village turn right onto a vehicle track and pass by a football pitch and a small school on your right. Continue along this track on the left hand side heading towards the V end of the canyon.

Photo: Looking back down the valley to Soccma

The vehicle track starts to disintegrate and head left and upwards. Pick up the footpath again that heads directly ahead and soon reach an obvious Inca stepped path that steeply climbs up to the base of the waterfall. The path isn't always obvious now, but at this point you will be able to hear the waterfall and make the best way through the trees to its base. This stunning waterfall is over 100m in height and the

moisture in the air provides an ideal environment for a variety of wild flowers and fruit shrubs.

Photo: The waterfall from higher on the path

The Inca ruins of Raqaypata are now directly above you on the clifftop. To reach them you must head slightly down, then pick up the path that continues on up and around the V of the canyon. The path is quite steep and when it splits there are two options: dip down and up to the right for a short cut, or continue up and around past the buildings and entrance.

Photo: Raqaypata

The site is being restored and the short cut path may be closed during the rainy season, or difficult to pass because of the construction works. It is best to take a view on the day according to the weather conditions and amount of activity at the site.

Once you have visited the site, continue out and along the path towards a rocky outcrop. The path turns sharp left here to go steeply uphill, before turning to the right, or alternately you can cut the corner off along a narrower faint path that re-joins the main path after a few hundred metres. The path continues to ascend gradually and following the valley where

Soccma is located down to your right. At approx. 18km the path finally reaches its highest point at the Mirador Pincuylluna, giving you an amazing view of the Sacred Valley below.

Photo: Mirador

Soon the path starts to descend and here you have the option of continuing down to the right towards Pachar, or down to the left to reach Ollantaytambo. Ollantaytambo is nearer and has better options for return transport, and many restaurants and cafes for post hike refreshments. Taking the route back to Pachar will pass through Cochana and Santa Ana and an opportunity to see the small Inca ruins, the *colqas*, and the Inca bridge, before crossing over into Pachar.

Finish point:	**Pachar or Ollantaytambo**
To return to Cusco:	Flag down any bus or collectivo heading to Cusco, or Urubamba bus terminal then take a bus or collectivo from Urubamba back to Cusco.

Walk Title:	**15. Señor de Huanca**
Summary:	Every year on 14th September thousands of people make this catholic pilgrimage route from Cusco to the sanctuary of Señor de Huanca, starting at 4am in order to arrive at the church in time for the service. Any other time of year, except for one or two locals, you'll have this path to yourself.
Elevation:	**Ascent** | **1,100m** | **Descent** | **1,100m** | **Maximum** | **4,270m**
Distance:	**15km**
Approx. time:	**8hrs**
Grading:	**Difficult – Medium if starting from Huaccoto**
Type:	**Linear**
Travelling time:	**20mins to San Jeronimo – 1hr return to Cusco**
Entrance fees:	**None**
Start point:	**San Jeronimo plaza**
To get to the start point:	Taxi to San Jeronimo plaza S/10 – If starting from Huaccoto, taxi to Huacotto from San Jeronimo S/25

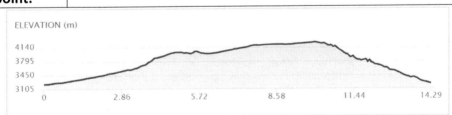

From the plaza walk to the top right hand corner of the church, along one block and turn left into Sorama. Walk up the street until you reach the end,

and directly opposite is the start of the route, marked by a yellow 'H' and an arrow. However, it is easier to turn right, go along the street for another 100m and turn left up the vehicle track. You should see a blue road sign for 'Huanca 40km' (this is by road). Head straight up this track and towards the end of the houses fork left. Shortly after see a small aqueduct across the stream on your left. At the junction continue uphill, signed by the yellow arrow.

At 1.5km the path splits, take the right path. Here there is another yellow arrow and the first Km01 small concrete post. The arrows and the Km markers signpost the route the whole way to Huanca, although they are patchy in some parts.

As you walk up this grassy path, you'll see some Inca ruins on the left which are not really worth the detour, this day is already long. After 500m reach a small reservoir and the arrow turns left to the road. Turn right along the road and after another few hundred metres pick up the path again at the next switchback. Do the same again when you next reach the road, you are just cutting off the zig-zags.

Just after 3km reach a sharp right hand bend with a couple of the yellow signs and arrows, and at the next corner see an arrow pointing sharp left. Here, leave the track and head up steeply on a faint path which soon becomes clearer and another yellow arrow confirms you are on the correct path.

Photo: View of Cusco

The path zig-zags steeply up the hill for another 2km, passing the corner of the vehicle track, and eventually meeting it at 5.2km. Turn right along the road and see the village of Huaccoto in front of you. You can follow the vehicle track around the bend, or cut off the corner through the field. If you are starting from Huaccoto, take a taxi to the village sign.

Photo: Approaching Huaccoto

After the village sign, keep on the track and pick up the path that runs up alongside the blue terraced houses. As you reach the end of the village the path runs up through a broad stream, veer right and walk up to the crest of the hill to find the cross.

From the cross head slightly left around the hillside and the path becomes wide and clear again. The path crosses the altiplano for a couple of kilometres, crossing a few small streams, until you reach the pass at 10.2km,

marked by several crosses. Just over the pass are some small Inca ruins, which make a good place to stop for a picnic, as you have stunning views down into the valley beyond.

Photo: View of the valley from just beyond the pass

As you start to descend you can see the red roof of the Sanctuary below you. The path descends steeply for 2km then becomes more gradual. Closer to the Sanctuary pass through some small Inca ruins, then cross over the road and go through the Holy Garden with the life-size holy figures reaching the Sanctuary church building at 14.5km.

The Sanctuary is busy on Sundays and it should be possible to find transport from here down to the village of San Salvador. On any other day it might be difficult, and you may have to walk a further 3km down into the village. Pick up the path down below the church after some red steps, and this goes all the way down to the main road. Turn right on the main road and walk alongside the river into the village until you reach the bridge.

Finish point:	Señor de Huanca Sanctuary or San Salvador
To return to Cusco:	Combis run from the bridge back to Cusco S/3

Walk Title:	16. Tambomachay to Huchuy Qosqo						
Summary:	This route follows an original Inca trail from the sacred spring of Tambomachay to the royal palace at Huchuy Qosqo. A long walk over the high Andean plains is rewarded with the final descent to Huchuy Qosqo through a beautiful canyon and valley.						
Elevation:	Ascent	760m	Descent	1,600m	Maximum	4,300m	
Distance:	23km						
Approx. time:	8hrs						
Grading:	Difficult						
Type:	Linear						
Travelling time:	20mins to start, 1 hour return from Lamay						
Entrance fees:	S/25						
Start point:	Tambomachay (3,800m)						
To get to the start point:	Tambomachay is on the outskirts of town as you leave the Sacsaywaman site. Take a taxi from the centre S/15, or take the Señor de Huerto bus to the final stop on its route S/1.20						

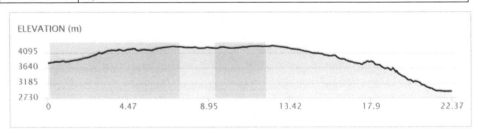

If you have a ticket for Tambomachay or intend to visit the site, then this walk starts at the far end near the springs. Cross the wooden bridge and head off to your left on the path.

Photo: The ruins of Tambomachay

If you don't have a ticket then you can start this walk just down the road from the entrance. Opposite the sign to Puka Pukara and one bus stop before, there is a dirt vehicle track which heads up into the village of Tambomachay. After 200m cut off the corner of the track and turn right at the little wooden refuse collection point. After 600m the road turns into footpath and you see the ruins of Tambomachay down to your right. Follow this path round until you see the bridge below you.

After 1.5km from the start, the path starts through scrub area and after another 200m you can see more Inca terraces to your left. Now the path continues on the right hand side of the valley, and after another 400m you should see a concrete water installation down to your left and an orange water pipe in the distance. The path starts to go sharply uphill, and here you must take care if you are walking in rainy season, since the water frequently washes the path away and makes it unclear. At the top cross over the channel for the water pipe and continue straight ahead, crossing a couple more dug water channels. Your general direction is to keep to the right hand side of the hill you are on.

On the other side, you should now be able to see a large bunch of jumbled rocks. Continue on and up your path, and soon you come level to the rocks, passing a rock marker on the path at 2.8km. After another 400m reach the top of the pass. On your left is a waymarker pile of stones and earth. You will see these frequently now along the high route. Look back for great views of Cusco. Here turn sharp left past the waymarker.

As you continue along the path, down to your left you will see young trees planted along irrigation channels, causing a plantation in a grid-like effect.

After another 500m reach the 2nd waymarker and pass over into a deep valley.

Photo: Valley back to Cusco

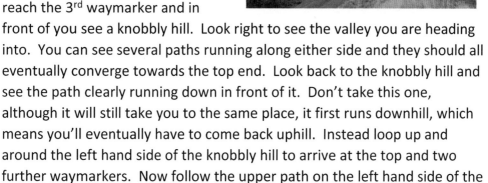

The path winds around the left hand side and is clear to see. At 4.3km reach the 3rd waymarker and in front of you see a knobbly hill. Look right to see the valley you are heading into. You can see several paths running along either side and they should all eventually converge towards the top end. Look back to the knobbly hill and see the path clearly running down in front of it. Don't take this one, although it will still take you to the same place, it first runs downhill, which means you'll eventually have to come back uphill. Instead loop up and around the left hand side of the knobbly hill to arrive at the top and two further waymarkers. Now follow the upper path on the left hand side of the valley, following the path parallel on the right hand side.

At 6.2km the path crosses the stream to the other side and in another 300m reach a waymarker where the path from the other side converges. The path now heads upwards on the right hand side of an altiplano, where you might see llama and sheep grazing. Outside of dry season there should be a small lake here. At 7.6km you reach another pass. Down below you, you should see a reservoir and a small dam.

Photo: Reservoir

This is where you are more likely to see herds of llama as they congregate around the water. There is a vehicle track which runs from the other side of the dam out towards the left.

Photo: Shepherdess on the pass

You are now in a natural bowl, and your general direction is to head from the bottom left hand corner to the top right hand corner. The clearest way is to head down over the dam, and pick up the vehicle track although this is the least scenic. A better way is to turn left hand side of the bowl. At a pass at the top left hand corner you are rewarded with amazing views down to Lake Piuray. Carry on round to the top right hand corner, over the small ridge and pick up the vehicle track. This track eventually runs all the way down to the community of Q'enqo. Now you are out of the bowl and over the ridge. In front of you there are some corrals on the hillside, and for reference you are midway between Lake Piuray on your left and Lake Quriqucha on your right.

Follow the vehicle track round and just above the corrals, pick up a footpath which swoops away to your left. It looks faint to start with but soon becomes more distinct. Distances recorded from now on may vary depending on which route you took.

Photo: Corrals on hillside

As you reach the top of another pass and another waymarker, you should see a series of electricity pylons running through the valley in front of you.

The path continues towards these and passes directly past the base of one of these. The path veers to the right and in 250m reach another waymarker. These frequently mark the path between here and the highest pass. From this waymarker look to the distance and see on the horizon the large rock markers of the pass. The path undulates and weaves across the plain for another 2km until you reach the rather elaborate pass. This part of the walk takes you across the most exposed area, and you should take care when walking in rainy season, as this area is susceptible to thunderstorms.

From the pass, the path down has been restored to its original state, wide and even, marking the approach to a royal residence. Continue down for another 2.3km to reach a small community Pucamarca, which looks deserted, but the few people that still live there are mainly shepherds and usually spend the day out on the hills. The path runs alongside the village for another 600m until you reach the familiar Inca walls at the first Inca control point for Huchuy Qosqo.

Head down the steps and round into the canyon and after 300m turn left down some more steps, cross the wooden bridge and head through the

second control point.

Photo: Second control point

The path continues through a narrow gorge and across a couple more bridges before opening out into a canyon. Continue along the path down the left hand side of both the canyon and the stream. The wooden bridges along the way are for sightseeing only. It is another 3km from the first control point to reach a mirador with a small shelter. Here, the path to the right will short cut straight to the path down, but misses out the Huchuy Qosqo site. To visit Huchuy Qosqo, continue in the same direction you came from for another 1km to arrive at one of the entrance gates to the site.   After a few metres see the sign directing towards Lamay. Pick this up when you are ready to exit. The ranger will find you for the entrance fee while you are exploring the site.

Photo: Inca terraces at Huchuy Qosqo

When you are ready to leave the site, return to the Lamay exit point and follow the path down.

After 1km you will meet the short-cut from the mirador, but otherwise there are no other options on the way down. It is 3.5km of switchbacks and fairly steep path. Take care in all seasons as the path can be slippery. For most of the way down, you can see the community this side of the river that you are heading towards, and you need to walk through here to cross the concrete bridge across the river. At the time of writing the road up through the village was being extended and so the path down had been re-routed to the near side of the village. It doesn't matter which path you take down to the village.

Cross the river and the route finishes at the main road, in the centre of Lamay.

Finish point:	Lamay
To return to Cusco:	The bus stop is immediately adjacent to the finish point. Buses to Cusco are approx. every 15 minutes – S/2, or hail a collectivo - S/5. A taxi all the way back to Cusco will cost S/35.

Bonus Chapter:	17. The Secret Way to Machu Picchu		
Summary:	For the time-rich money-poor traveller, this chapter tells you how to travel to Machu Picchu for just $10		
Elevation:	Ascent	Descent	Maximum
Distance:	240km		
Approx. time:	8-12hrs		
Grading:	Easy		
Entrance fees:			
Start point:	Cusco		

Aguas Calientes, otherwise known as Machu Picchu town, is situated in the high jungle and in the valley below Machu Picchu. It is only accessible by train, or foot, and it exists purely to service the 1 million tourists that visit Machu Picchu every year. The town itself is very unexciting, a collection of hostels and hotels, restaurants and souvenir shops and stalls and it is best visited as a stopover only for visiting the citadel of the Incan Empire.

There are some hot springs (from which the town takes its name) open to the public at the top end of town and these are usually busy from mid-afternoon onwards as the trekkers finishing the Inca Trail route soak their aching limbs. Towels can be rented for about S/5 from a couple of places on the way up to the springs. Admission is S/20 for tourists, and S/5 for Peruvians.

Many tourists travel to Aguas Calientes by train either from Poroy, near Cusco, or Ollantaytambo. The sole operator, Peru Rail, offers return tickets for various prices ranging from $120 on a first train out, last train back basis, to $900 to travel on the 5-star Hiram Bingham train. The trains are also used to transport goods to the town, and there is usually one coach at the back for locals to use. Kilometre for kilometre, it is a very expensive route to travel.

Many agencies in Cusco offer a minibus round trip to Hidroelectrica, dropping you off from 2pm onwards, and collecting you late the next day. The price will vary according to agency and season, but expect to pay from S/90/$30. The route is the same as explained below.

Total time for this trip is:

Time in vehicle 6hrs + walking time 3hrs = 9hrs

It is recommended that you are on the road out of Cusco before 9am, as you don't want to be walking the last part in the dark. This route is becoming more popular with travellers wanting a cheaper alternative to reaching Machu Picchu than the train, and waiting time for collectivos to fill up is fairly short between legs. We last travelled this route in February, low season, and waited a maximum of 20 minutes for a collectivo to fill.

1. Cusco to Santa Maria – 200km

Buses and collectivos both leave from the same street Ave Antonio Lorena, close to the cemetery. They head towards Quillabamba but you get off about three quarters of the way there at Santa Maria.

Buses

The buses run from the station Terminal Terrestre de Quillabamba. There are a few companies that run the route several times during the day and most have a bus leaving early in the morning. A one-way ticket can cost as little as S/15 if you sit in the front seats, rising to S/50 nearer the back in the more luxurious seats. Most buses have a toilet on-board. It is best to check the timetable the day before. Approx. time is 5 hours.

Collectivos

It is impossible not to be aware of this service. As soon as you arrive on Ave Antonio Lorena people will be calling and shouting for you to join their collective minibus or car. Cost is S/30 per person, but you might be able to negotiate it down to S/25 to take the last seat, or if there is a group of you. We used Campana situated on Valle Inka/Trés Marias just behind the bus station, as they have a good safety record. Collectivos are quicker and take only 4 hours.

2. Santa Maria to Santa Theresa – 22km

Santa Maria is a village on the main road through to Quillabamba. There are a few local restaurants and tiendas to buy snacks, and some fruit stalls along the roadside. Quillabamba is still in high jungle, but is the beginning of the fruit, cacao, coffee and tea growing area. All collectivos and buses stop in the centre of Santa Maria village, and you simply cross the road to pick up the next collectivo towards Santa Theresa. Cost is S/10 per person and its approx. 45 minutes to 1 hour depending on the state of the road and the season you're travelling in. Buses do not cover this route.

3. Santa Theresa to Hidroelectrica – 7km

Santa Theresa is a pretty little village, best known for its hot springs which are slightly further on and down by the river. If you have a spare couple of hours, they really are worth a visit, as they are cleaner, clearer and much less crowded than those at Aguas Calientes.

On arrival at Santa Theresa the collectivo will drop you at the top of the village, and this is the place where you will change to take the next collectivo towards Hidroelectrica. Cost is S/5 and time is approx. 40 minutes. About 5 minutes before Hidroelectrica is the entrance to the National Park and the driver will wait for any tourists in the vehicle to go and sign in. You will need your passport or identity card to register, but entrance is free.

The end of the road will be obvious, a big turning point and car park with collectivos and minibuses arriving and departing. Walk along the train tracks and Hidroelectrica station and some trackside tiendas are here.

4. Hidroelectrica to Aguas Calientes – 11km

From this point to Aguas Calientes is either by train or walking.

Tickets for the train can be purchased at the ticket office here, one-way S/100 with approx. 4 departures a day, and takes less than an hour.

If you are walking the route, simply follow the tracks out of the station. At the beginning there are 3 switchback tracks for the train to navigate a steep section, but the walking path cuts across those and is actually signposted for you towards Aguas Calientes. Once you have reached this signpost, the route is a more gradual incline, and there is a continual path on the side of the tracks. It should be noted that the Peruvian government does not promote or support the method of walking along the tracks. There are many signs telling you not to do it, and this is because there is always one person every year who gets killed while they were walking along the middle of the tracks with headphones in their ears listening to music. Be sensible, use the path, listen out for the trains, and move well away from the track when they pass, and all will be well.

From Hidroelectrica to Aguas Calientes is the uphill route, a change in altitude of 400m, and takes about 3 hours. It is a pleasant walk with the river below, and the mountains beyond, and there are one or two places where it's possible to see Machu Picchu above perched on the hillside. There are also a few places to buy food, snacks and water along the way, but the prices are premium.

The path comes into the bottom of the town and joins the road up to the centre. About 1km from town you'll pass the bridge across the river where the path up to Machu Picchu starts.

5. Aguas Calientes to Machu Picchu archaeological site

There are many agencies who will try to sell you a day tour to Machu Picchu either in Cusco or once you have reached Aguas Calientes. Unless you want someone to look after the administration for you, it is unnecessary. Entrance tickets can be bought online from www.machupicchu.gob.pe or from the kiosk situated in the corner of the plaza in the town. The availability is limited to 2,500 tickets per day so buying them in advance is recommended if you are travelling during high season. Prices are shown on the website.

The entrance ticket does not include the cost of the bus that transports you from Aguas Calientes town up the mountain to the main entrance of the archaeological site, which will cost a further $24 per person return journey. Of course, the alternative is to walk up the path that leads from the bridge to the site entrance on top of the mountain. It is a boring uphill walk, the path has many uneven steps and traverses the switchback route the bus takes. It's an ascent of 400m takes about 2 hours. Take plenty of water and insect repellent.

Photo: Machu Picchu

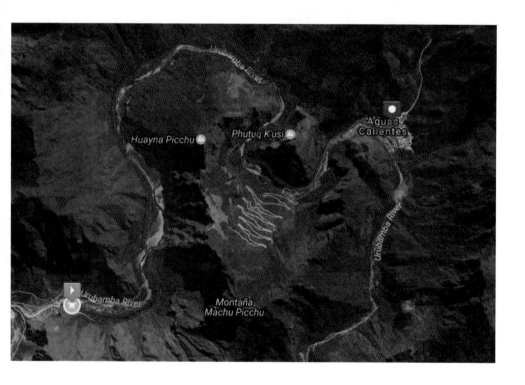

Inca sites and other places of interest

The following are a brief guide to the Inca sites and other places of interest visited on these walks. It is only intended to give a flavour of the site, for more detailed information and history of these sites, it is recommended that you obtain a guide book of the local area. The Incas did not record any history in writing, and so there are always several interpretations and suggestions as to what were the origins or purpose of a site. It is possible, while you are in Peru, that you will hear several historical variations.

Cachiccata is visible from the sun temple at Ollantaytambo and sits between 700 and 900 metres above the valley floor. There are 3 quarries within ½ km of each other and it was from here that the great stone blocks were transported to Ollantaytambo, by sliding them first down the hillside and then floating them across the river. There are many half-finished blocks littered around the sites, with the last quarry containing the mysterious needle-shaped stones.

Chinchero is believed to have been the estate of the son of the Inca king Pachacuteq. These days it is visited more for its markets and traditional textiles. The best market is held in the market square on a Sunday when it is possible to buy fresh fruit and vegetables from the nearby farms, and a range of handicrafts. There are a number of weaving centres in the town where you can see an interesting demonstration of the whole process from raw wool to finished woven product.

Huchuy Qosqo was a presidential palace built for the 8th Inca king, Viracocha, and stands on a plateau overlooking the Urubamba valley. When the Chanka people from the Ayacucho region, known for their ferocity, attacked the Incas in Cusco, Viracocha abandoned his people to their fate and retreated to his palace with his close family. Shortly after this, he was overthrown and one of the most famous Inca kings – Pachacuteq – came to power. Part stone, part adobe, the complex is partially restored but receives few visitors, mainly due to its inaccessibility.

Inkilltambo is a religious site originally created by the Pre-Inca Ayarmaca, who occupied the region around 1,000 years ago. It has a large central rock with small carved enclosures where mummies were placed. The remains of a ritual bath can be seen at the base, and at the equinoxes the sun sets in the centre of the fissures on top.   It was later used by the Incas for the mummies of important dignitaries.

Ñaupa Iglesia is a *waka* hidden in the hills just outside of the small village of Pachar. It is a beautifully carved altar with a recess on the face of the boulder. On the sides of the recess are three steps.   The steps represent the three levels of the Andean world: The lower or underworld (the Ukhu Pacha), the middle world or the world we live in (the Kay Pacha) and the upper or celestial world (the Hanan Pacha). Behind the altar is a cave with precisely carved doorways, usually with offerings placed in them.

Ollantaytambo is a town and Inca archaeological site in the Sacred Valley. During the Inca Empire, Ollantaytambo was the royal estate of Pachacuti who conquered the region and built the town with a ceremonial centre. When the Spanish invaded it served as a stronghold for Yupanqui, leader of the Inca resistance. Nowadays tourists are attracted by the Inca buildings and as the starting point for the Inca Trail.

Puca Pucara translates to Red Fort, although it was most likely a lodging house for travellers, perhaps to visit the nearby springs at Tambomachay.

Pumamarca sits at a strategic point a few kilometres outside of Ollantaytambo. From this site it's possible to see in many directions and for this reason was a soldiers' outpost, the first defence against attack at the important town. Invaders would have to breach this fort first before funnelling down the small valley to the town's defended walls.

Qenqo is a *waka*, a worshipping site. Inside the natural rock is what looks like a carved altar. The niches were used to bury mummies and offerings of gold and other objects. Qenqo means zig-zag, and the numerous zig-zag carvings are undoubtedly what gave it its name. To the edge of the rock are the remains of a carved puma and condor.

Qhapaq Ñan was the principal 6,000km royal road which joined the cities of Quito, Ecuador to the north and Santiago, Chile in the south and allowed the Inca to control their Empire sending troops as needed from the capital, Cusco. Along the route were warehouses, relay stations, llama corrals, living quarters and military posts.

Sacsayhuaman is the largest and most important Inca site in the area and stands on the hillside to the north of the city. Now reduced to just the enormous outer walls since most of the smaller stones were removed for use in the construction of the houses and palaces in Cusco for the Spanish *conquistadors* in the 16th century. Sacsayhuaman had a variety of uses, from garrison of some 5,000 troops, to a religious site, to an administrative centre. It was the site of a huge rebellion between the Manco Inca and the Spanish in 1536, in which despite being hopelessly outnumbered, the Spanish gained victory, slaughtering thousands of Inca in the process.

Tambomachay is popularly referred to as the Inca's Bath, this well preserved site was for ritual bathing for the important Inca dignitaries. Three stone water courses are fed by a natural spring from the hillside. Some guides will tell you that the Inca believed the waters had healing and immortality properties.

The Temple of the Moon (Templo de la Luna) is a natural rock which is the largest *waka* in the area. Using the two caves within it, the Inca also carved various intricate animals into its surface, predominantly puma and snakes, most of which were partly destroyed by the invading Spanish. Inside the biggest cave are niches for mummies and an altar, which catches the full moon on a winter solstice.

The Temple of the Monkey (Templo del Mono) is also part of the greater Sacsaywaman complex. Also known as Kusilluchayoq it is still a sacred place today, where you will see offerings of flowers and seeds from recent rituals and ceremonies. You'll need to look closely to see the monkeys carved into the rock face, and the carved puma which again were defaced by the Spanish invaders.

The Sacred Valley is the general area referred to between the towns of Pisac and Ollantaytambo. The Urubamba river (also known as the Vilcanota) runs through the valley, and the fertile river plains on either side were (and still are) the agricultural centre of the Inca Empire, producing much of the staple vegetables for the city of Cusco. The main crop is corn, also the biggest export of the region. The valley has many Inca sites as well as the familiar agricultural terracing throughout the region. It is simply a stunning landscape too, the granite mountains reaching some 500-600m to either side of the river floor.

Glossary

abra	Summit
altiplano	A high altitude plain
canteras	Quarries
chicha	A slightly alcoholic drink brewed with corn, available to buy in the street, or in villages where you see a flag outside a property
chullpas	Burial towers
collectivo	A shared taxi or minibus. Passengers pay a single fare and wait for the vehicle to fill up
combi	Small busses that run on local town/city routes
corral	Stone enclosure for animals
final	The final stop on a combi route
Instituto Nacional Cultura (INC)f3333	National Cultural Institute – The government body responsible for the archaeological sites
paradero	Bus stop
taxista	Taxi driver
tienda	Small shop selling basic groceries
waka	Worshipping site or temple

Made in the USA
Lexington, KY
13 March 2017